American Woodies
1928-1953

Those were the days ...

Also from Veloce –

Those Were The Days ... Series
Alpine Trials & Rallies 1910-1973 (Pfundner)
American 'Independent' Automakers – AMC to Willys 1945 to 1960 (Mort)
American Station Wagons – The Golden Era 1950-1975 (Mort)
American Trucks of the 1950s (Mort)
American Trucks of the 1960s (Mort)
American Woodies 1928-1953 (Mort)
Anglo-American Cars from the 1930s to the 1970s (Mort)
Austerity Motoring (Bobbitt)
Austins, The last real (Peck)
Brighton National Speed Trials (Gardiner)
British Lorries of the 1950s (Bobbitt)
British Lorries of the 1960s (Bobbitt)
British Touring Car Racing (Collins)
British Police Cars (Walker)
British Woodies (Peck)
Café Racer Phenomenon, The (Walker)
Dune Buggy Phenomenon, The (Hale)
Dune Buggy Phenomenon Volume 2, The (Hale)
Endurance Racing at Silverstone in the 1970s & 1980s (Parker)
Hot Rod & Stock Car Racing in Britain in the 1980s (Neil)
Last Real Austins 1946-1959, The (Peck)
MG's Abingdon Factory (Moylan)
Motor Racing at Brands Hatch in the Seventies (Parker)
Motor Racing at Brands Hatch in the Eighties (Parker)
Motor Racing at Crystal Palace (Collins)
Motor Racing at Goodwood in the Sixties (Gardiner)
Motor Racing at Nassau in the 1950s & 1960s (O'Neil)
Motor Racing at Oulton Park in the 1960s (McFadyen)
Motor Racing at Oulton Park in the 1970s (McFadyen)
Superprix – The Story of Birmingham Motor Race (Page & Collins)
Three Wheelers (Bobbitt)

Truckmakers
DAF Trucks since 1949 (Peck)

General
Micro Trucks (Mort)

From Veloce's new imprints –

Soviet General & field rank officer uniforms: 1955 to 1991 (Streather)
Red & Soviet military & paramilitary services: female uniforms 1941-1991 (Streather)

A comprehensive guide for the Trainee Dog Groomer (Gould)
A dog's dinner (Paton-Ayre)
Animal Grief (Alderton)
Bramble: the dog who wanted to live forever (Heritage)
Cat Speak (Rauth-Widmann)
Clever Dog! (O'Meara)
Complete Dog Massage Manual, The – Gentle Dog Care (Robertson)
Dinner with Rover (Paton-Ayre)
Dog Cookies – Healthy allergen-tree treat recipes for your dog (Schops & Pick)
Dog Games – Stimulating play to entertain your dog and you (Blenski)
Dog Relax – Relaxed dogs, relaxed owners (Pilguj)
Dog Speak (Blenski)
Dogs on wheels (Mort)
Emergency first aid for dogs (Bucksch)
Exercising your puppy: a gentle & natural approach – Gentle Dog Care (Robertson & Pope)
Know your dog – The guide to a beautiful relationship (Birmelin)
Living with an Older Dog – Gentle Dog Care (Alderton & Hall)
My dog has cruciate ligament injury – but lives life to the full! (Häusler)
My dog has hip dysplasia – but lives life to the full! (Häusler)
My dog is blind – but lives life to the full! (Horsky)
Smellorama! – Nose games for dogs (Theby)
Swim to Recovery: Canine hydrotherapy healing – Gentle Dog Care (Wong)
Waggy Tails & Wheelchairs (Epp)
Walkin' the dog – Motorway walks for dogs and drivers (Rees)
Winston ... the dog who changed my life (Klute)
You and Your Border Terrier – The Essential Guide (Alderton)
You and Your Cockapoo – The Essential Guide (Alderton)

www.velocebooks.com

First published in November 2010 by Veloce Publishing Limited, Veloce House, Parkway Farm Business Park, Middle Farm Way, Poundbury, Dorchester, Dorset, DT1 3AR, England. Fax 01305 250479/e-mail info@veloce.co.uk/web www.veloce.co.uk or www.velocebooks.com.

ISBN: 978-1-845842-69-7 UPC: 6-36847-04269-1

© Norm Mort and Veloce Publishing 2010. All rights reserved. With the exception of quoting brief passages for the purpose of review, no part of this publication may be recorded, reproduced or transmitted by any means, including photocopying, without the written permission of Veloce Publishing Ltd. Throughout this book logos, model names and designations, etc, have been used for the purposes of identification, illustration and decoration. Such names are the property of the trademark holder as this is not an official publication. Readers with ideas for automotive books, or books on other transport or related hobby subjects, are invited to write to the editorial director of Veloce Publishing at the above address. British Library Cataloguing in Publication Data – A catalog record for this book is available from the British Library. Typesetting, design and page make-up all by Veloce Publishing Ltd on Apple Mac. Printed in India by Replika Press.

Contents

Acknowledgements 4
Introduction 6
In the beginning ... early American woodies 1886-1927 8
1928-1931: Ford leads the way! 12
American woodies – an emerging market: 1932-1942 19
American woodies – the finest and last: 1945-1953 50
Woodies today 88

Index 91

Acknowledgements

This is the eighth book I've written in conjunction with my son, Andrew. His photographic skills have once again revealed the often flamboyant and unique styling of the American woody station wagons, convertibles and sedans.

These chic, yet often seen as dual-purpose woody designs were dubbed 'Station Wagons', and were used by owners of country estates or inns for picking up guests and lodgers arriving by rail. These gleaming wooden vehicles were also aimed towards the well-to-do sportsman and high-society crowd.

Woodies were custom-built by specialists such as Ionia-Mitchell, Hercules, Cantrell, US Body and Forging, etc, for specific American automakers, and in a wide range of models, sizes and designs.

A favorite vehicle in American films of the period, today the woody is a prize addition to any collection, and appeals to a dedicated group of collectors and enthusiasts worldwide.

As well as my enthusiasm and fascination with these classic American vehicles, and my son Andrew's photographic talents, this book would not have been possible without the encouragement, kindness and co-operation of many others.

Many of the advertisement and brochure images, as well as some photos, were provided through the kindness of fellow Canadian authors and automotive historians Thomas McPherson and Walt McCall, and keen Walter P Chrysler club member Bill Filbert.

A number of generous woody enthusiasts provided images of their Woodies. These included collector Paul Jenkins (1946 Chrysler Town & Country Sedan), Harold Mermel (1942 Chrysler Town & Country 'Barrelback' and 1950 Chrysler Town & Country Sedan), Dale Morse (1938 Dodge ½-ton Commercial), Jack Huiberts (1950 Dodge Coronet Wagon), Glenn Johnson (1928 Ford Model A Wagon), Arthur Goldstone (1946 Mercury & 1948 Chevy Wagons), Edwin L 'Brownie' Petersen, (1951 Chevrolet), Bill Spear, President of the Austin Bantam Society provided images of members cars (1938-41 Bantam Woodies), Christopher Lawrence (1937 Dodge Westchester Suburban), Don Bryant (1947 Chevrolet woody Suburban), W. Peters (1933 Chevrolet), Albert & Kathryn Golden (1947 Pontiac Streamliner Wagon), Tom Jeffris' (1946 Oldsmobile submitted by friend Tim Sheridan), Scott and Damian Melcer (1950 DeSoto woody Wagon), Henri David Jr (1947 Plymouth Special DeLuxe and 1948 Chevrolet Fleetmaster), Carl Stoutenberg (1936 Chevrolet), Bob Jacoveet & Fred Ruetz (1940 Chevrolet), David Goss (1946 Ford Sportsman & 1924 Model T Ford), Mimi Halgren (Studebaker Driver's Club), and Dean Lundblad (1948 Chevy Wagon, back cover).

A number of fine American car clubs were also invaluable in putting us in touch with their avid membership, whose input really added to this book, and for which we are very grateful. These included Ian Smale and other fine folks at the Chrysler Town & Country Owners Registry, c/o the WPC (Walter P Chrysler Club); Dan O'Day, Rich Barbaria and many

Preface

'Woody' station wagons were very popular with film stars; this 1940 Buick Super, Model 59, was later owned by Academy Award winning actress Bette Davis. One of just 495 Estate Wagons built that year by Buick, it featured a body built by the Biehl Body Company of Reading, PA. It was purchased originally by the Warner Brothers studio, and appeared in various big Hollywood films such as *George Washington Slept Here*, *White Heat*, and *Now Voyager* before being given to Bette Davis. (Andrew Mort)

others with the super keen VCCA (Vintage Chevrolet Club of America); the ISWC (International Station Wagon Club) President and Editor, Chuck Snyder; Pete Philips of the Buick Club of America; and John Lee editor of the *Woodie Times* of the National Woodie Club, as well as the Model A Ford Club of America.

Andrew and I would also once again like to thank Rod Grainger of Veloce Publishing.

As part of the popular Those were the days ... series from Veloce Publishing, *American Woodies 1928-1953* is a highly visual study with over 120 images focusing on the rise in popularity of the stylish 'woody' station wagons and evolving sedans and convertibles in North America from the introduction of the Ford Model A in 1928 through to 1953 when the last woody was officially built by Buick. Although occasionally some references are made to the many commercial, Canopy Express, panel trucks, Hucksters, professional cars, and buses, etc fitted with wooden bodies, this volume in no way attempts to cover these vehicles. Nor does it attempt to include the rare one-off wooden custom-bodied cars built or the various post-war woody national auto show cars such as those built by Lincoln in 1955.

5

Introduction

Wood had been a universal material in automobile and truck body construction dating back to the first horseless carriages. Yet it was a material that required considerable time, craftsmanship and maintenance. Steel panels that could be quickly stamped out and painted were far more practical and helped speed-up production, although safety was stressed by the automobile manufacturers in the advertising of the day.

Still, wood was to remain a fundamental element in automobile construction into the 1930s – and in fact right into the 1960s wood was used for floors, convertible top headers, etc. Today, of course, real wood is relegated to rich interior trim.

But wood required time-consuming craftsmanship, and didn't have the long term durability, overall strength and speedy production efficiency of steel.

Despite this, vehicle manufacturers realized a wood finish and the blending of various shades of woods and grains had a highly appealing, eye-catching style. It was also ideal for limited production models for niche markets. As a result, automobile and truck manufacturers were very willing to offer a rolling chassis to customers, to fit a body constructed of wood to whatever specifications and special needs they might require, or offer a line of special production models.

Henry Ford's success and domination of the woody station wagon market began with his introduction of the stylish Model A woody wagon late in 1928. Its great appeal, and higher volume in-house production soon caught the attention of competing American automobile manufacturers big and small.

Often the most exclusive and expensive models in the line-up; soon, as well as woody station wagons, America's automakers by the 1940s and into the fifties began offering woody sedans, two-door hardtops and

It was Henry and Edsel Ford with their Model A that really established the station wagon as a popular model with the public in general. This fine example was one of only five built in 1928. (Courtesy Glenn Johnson)

Between 1928 and 1953, American woody station wagons were built by many different companies and in many different sizes, from truck-based 4x4s, such as this postwar K-Series International, to the tiny four-cylinder models like the 1938 American Bantam parked alongside. (Courtesy Bill Spear)

Preface

convertibles. Whereas the woody station wagons were initially designed for functionality with a high degree of style, the spawned woody sedans, hardtops and convertibles were constructed purely for style and pizzazz.

Adorned by wood along the flanks, and across the trunk of exterior bodywork with rich, polished woods lining the interiors, these highly fashionable wagons, sedans, hardtops and convertibles became a favourite of film stars, sportsmen and high society types. Such was the popularity of the woody look that large dealers sometimes arranged for a local furniture maker, or carpentry shop, to supply a trim kit for many of the popular sedan and convertible models, if the style was not offered by the factory.

American Woodies – 1928-1953 is not intended to be the definitive volume on these fine automobiles, but rather, provide an extensive line-up of the various models offered over that 25 year period. It is impossible to include an example of every woody constructed, so what we have here is a broad sampling of models by American car manufacturers, while also providing some insight into the building, marketing and history of the model.

Detailed captions, supportive text, contemporary brochure illustrations, period literature, factory photos and well over 50 new, unpublished colour photos of restored examples convey the importance of these historic vehicles, prized by collectors today.

Note: Production figures were researched extensively and varied greatly, depending on the source, and should be regarded as an educated estimate.

While high-society saw a certain charm and style in woody station wagons, there was a functionality that appealed to the trades, commercial outlets, farmers,

sportsmen and photographers, etc. This photograph of American sportsman, landscape and wildlife watercolorist and commercial photographer, James Lawrence, was taken in 1943 after a successful pheasant hunt in Orland, California. He had purchased his Dodge Westminster Suburban new in 1937. (Courtesy Christopher Lawrence)

Whether it was in two-door hardtop or convertible guise, the 1950 Chrysler Town and Country was a style leader. (Courtesy Tom McPherson)

In the beginning ... early American woodies 1886-1927

It was only natural that the first production cars built were constructed of wood. Many of the bodies of automobiles were built in wagon works and, as the horseless carriage proved itself, these companies and custom coachbuilders turned to automobile production.

These early automobiles were, of course, just buggies, coaches and wagons with a motor replacing the horse, but with the passage of time things changed quickly.

Speeds never dreamed of before, unless your horses got away from you, were achieved, and thus better protection from the elements and improved roadways were required. Other industries and businesses were needed to provide fuels, parts, service, etc. The age of the automobile had dawned.

The traditional wagon maker was soon eclipsed by the coachbuilder. In the beginning, custom bodywork was supplied to automobile inventors and builders only, due to very limited production.

What is today considered by many to be the first modern automobile came from Gottlieb Daimler in 1886. His gasoline engine and drive gear were fitted in coachwork he had ordered from a builder who had no idea why Daimler was insisting that strength and durability were the key points.

Carriage builders such as Massachusetts' Currier and Cameron built the body for the original Stanley brothers' steamer in 1894. That scenario was soon common throughout the eastern and mid-western United States, as many well established coachbuilders simply began developing new bodystyles to fit on the steel automobile chassis.

Although many of these prominent, well established coachbuilders – as well as a flood of newcomers built bodies for the luxury models being offered, the greater volume producers of the day, such as Ford, Oldsmobile, Rambler, Stanley and scores of others, began to build their own wooden bodies.

It is widely accepted that Daimler again led the way in a new concept for body construction. Wilhelm Maybach, while working for Daimler, designed the first Mercedes model in 1901. It was unique in its day for being the first automobile to have its engine up-front, with a gleaming radiator and covered by a metal hood. This is disputed by many who feel the American Victor steam car of 1900 was actually the first automobile to have metal panels on its wooden frame and was advertised as such: "... Every part of the carriage is metal, except the seat and the floorboards."

Regardless, more metal was now being used in new automobile body designs, and American E R Thomas unveiled his metal-bodied model in 1903. Although a wooden framework was still being utilized,

In the beginning ... early American woodies 1886-1927

it soon became very apparent that metal on a wooden frame was cheaper, lighter, easier and quicker. Even the traditional coachbuilders soon abandoned the all-wooden body in favour of wooden-framed bodies with steel fenders.

Early American luxury auto-builder Pierce-Arrow offered a body with cast aluminum incorporated as early as 1905. Interestingly, it was Pierce-Arrow that would first coin the term 'station wagon' in 1911.

The turning point in further reducing the amount of wood in car bodies occurred in the early 1920s. The Budd Manufacturing Company is accredited with building the first all-steel enclosed bodies for Dodge, and soon this type of construction became a standard throughout the industry.

Still, wood found favour in both large and small truck bodies for commercial use where customers had very specific needs for the delivery of goods or passengers. Wood could be easily shaped, although the cost of dyes and stampings was expensive unless used for a higher volume vehicle.

Thus, in many cases, local furniture or cabinetry shops built wooden bodies on chassis supplied by a dealer. Some sold a wooden body to dealers in knocked-down form for final assembly.

Production was limited and the designs often crude, although it depended on the talents of the shop owners, and some surviving examples display both fine lines and considerable ingenuity in design.

The 'Depot Hack' was usually built on a commercial chassis based on what was termed an 'Express truck.' Taking a train was the most common way to travel at this time, but when you arrived at the station there was no way to get to your final destination.

What is considered by most to be the world's first modern automobile was built by Gottlieb Daimler. It was a woody. How's that for heritage ... albeit not using that much wood! (Author's collection)

These full hardtop trucks were fitted with additional seats to transport railway passengers from the train depot to the big hotels in cities, or inns and lodges in the country.

Speciality firms were also being set up which catered specifically to certain companies and offered standard wooden bodies for delivery vehicles, station wagons or depot hacks, or for the larger station buses.

Not surprisingly, at this time, the most popular chassis for constructing depot hacks was the Ford Model T. It was readily available, and the cost for a running chassis averaged around $285 FOB Detroit.

As America grew so did the train depots that became busier and thus required more and more station wagons to transport passengers. Greater demand for station wagons meant greater production, and automobile manufacturers began shipping chassis directly to dealers or companies for the fitting of wooden station wagon bodies.

By definition the depot hacks and evolving station wagons were vehicles built on a production automobile, or smaller commercial (truck) chassis; fitted with a squared-off varnished or painted wooden body from the A-pillars back, and designed to carry seven to nine passengers, plus luggage. The roof was most often solid and there were at least three rows of seats or opposing rear bench seats. Weather protection consisted of roll-down side curtains.

By the late 1920s there were a large number of well established station wagon or 'Suburban' builders in the United States. Hercules, Mifflinburg and Cantrell were already names synonymous in the industry when it came to station wagons. Other prominent firms included York, Cotton, Martin-Parry, Baker-Raulang, and Seaman.

These companies often used a wide variety of terms, phrases and model names to describe their woodies and broaden market use. Estate Wagons, Suburban and Country Club models were "... the perfect vehicle for winter vacations in the southern states."

As a result of the expanding, upscale market towards personal use station wagons, creature comforts were enhanced throughout the 1920s. Better weather protection, four doors for easier entry and exit, and car-like comfort became expectations.

The first production woody station wagon is accredited to Durant in 1923, built on a standard chassis. The four-cylinder Star competed with the Model T Ford, although it never really challenged the industry leader. The Stoughton Wagon Company and Martin-Parry supplied the varnished wooden bodies which were shipped to the factory to be fitted and then shipped to the dealers. Production totals for the Star woody station wagon are unknown. Total Star and Durant model production was 105,288 units in 1923, but it's thought only a handful were station wagons. This, too, was a company high, production-wise, that would not be equaled. In fact, by the end in 1932 overall Durant production was down to a measly 1135 cars.

During the 1920s station wagon bodies were being offered on dozens of other American automakers' chassis, including the more popular makes such as Dodge, Overland, Chevrolet, Maxwell, REO, Essex and Buick. Buick offered three different models of its Passenger/Express woody. Although some companies utilized its truck chassis for a station wagon, the trend was toward using a larger car chassis.

In the last few years of the 1920s the styling of the woody station wagon also changed. As well as becoming even more car-like in comfort, the windows were now set in frames, and the side curtains spring-loaded for easy and fast operation when the weather changed. The doors were larger, while the windshields were smaller, and the side panels higher for greater protection.

The woody station wagon market continued to expand and Henry Ford was well aware of this fact. With the end of Model T production in 1927 and the introduction of the Model A in 1928, Ford was set to offer its own production woody station wagon.

In the beginning ... early American woodies 1886-1927

The body supplier is unknown for this rare 1926 Chevrolet woody Wagon. (Author's collection)

This restored 1924 Ford Model T woody was originally used by a Delaware butcher to haul meat, not passengers. (Courtesy David Goss)

1928-1931: Ford leads the way!

The Ford Motor Company was the largest vehicle manufacturer in the world, but by the time that Model T production ended in 1927, the company was being challenged by its competitors – particularly Chevrolet in North America. Sales in 1927 were down almost 450,000 units from the Model T's all-time high in 1923. Meanwhile, Chevrolet production had increased in 1927 by nearly thirty per cent and surpassed Ford in sales. Ford's overall US market share had slipped from forty-eight per cent to thirty per cent by 1926.

Thus, after nineteen years of production, the Model T gave way to the all-new Model A Ford.

The excitement of a new Ford car being unveiled swept the nation. It was an advertising and promotional dream. On December 2, 1927, 10,534,992 people, or nearly ten per cent of the American population, swarmed to dealer showrooms, large hotels, convention halls, and assembly plants to catch a glimpse of the new Ford for 1928.

Over the next few days it was estimated that almost a quarter of the population had seen the new Model A in the flesh.

The new Ford production station wagon based on the Model A chassis was not yet offered, but the decision was soon made to do so, and prototypes were developed in mid 1928 to show Henry Ford.

Henry Ford liked the design and saw merit in offering a station wagon model in the line-up. The decision was made to build more and debut it at the New York Auto Show early in 1929.

Five were built by the end of that year, differing slightly in construction to those that would appear later in 1929.

The biggest difference was the overall construction of the wooden body. Whereas the 1929 Model A Ford production station wagons featured finger joints, these first five woody wagons were constructed using lap joints.

Late in 1928 Ford built five pre-production Model A station wagon models. This rare, beautifully restored survivor is owned by enthusiast Glenn Johnson. The firewall date is 12/10/28, making it the earliest of the three 1928 woodies existing today. (Courtesy Glenn Johnson)

The construction and design of the 1928 Ford woody wagons were slightly different from the regular production models offered in 1929. Note the use of lap joints. (Courtesy Glenn Johnson)

1928-1931: Ford leads the way!

Ford's much anticipated Model A was the darling of America. Regardless of whether you were a businessman, a family man or a movie star, you lined up to order the new Ford. The woody was one of a number of all-new production models offered in 1929. (Author's collection)

American Woodies

Competition in the marketplace by 1930, chiefly from Chevrolet and Plymouth, forced Ford to restyle his Model A just two years later. Chains covered by leather sleeves supported the rear tailgate which, as Ford put it "... makes a splendid luggage deck because of its adequate size and sturdy construction." (Author's collection)

These 1928 Model A woody station wagons were also fitted with the early drum-shaped tail light, the late 1928 generator, fluted glass headlight lenses, and the fan shroud, while the handbrake was placed ahead of the gearshift lever.

Meanwhile, a complete chassis had also been offered from the start for $325 FOB Detroit. Outside companies were ready to fabricate station wagon body designs for the new Ford, but Ford introduced its own production version, known as the 150-A Station Wagon, in January 1929.

The price was $695, making the woody wagon one of the more expensive new 1929 Ford cars, yet it was initially advertised in its commercial catalogs.

It featured seating for eight, with the two rear seats being removable. Apparently, dealers had to be reminded initially to stress that this fashionable-looking wagon was also ideal for utility use by all sorts of trades people.

Ford set the tone with its woody station wagons. These were not the usual working vehicles of 1930, as can be seen in the dress of the owners and passengers; not to mention the chauffeur! (Author's collection)

The driver's compartment of the new 1930 Ford station wagon could accommodate three people. Tools were stored under this seat. "As a passenger conveyance it accommodates eight persons, with ample space for luggage …" (Author's collection)

The two rows of rear seating featured deep cushion seats covered in two-tone artificial leather. These could be removed for hauling large items with additional space provided by lowering the tailgate. (Author's collection)

www.velocebooks.com
Information on all books • New book news • Special offers • Gift vouchers

1928-1931: Ford leads the way!

The windscreen of the 1930 Model A station wagon was made of Triplex shatter-proof glass. This illustration shows all the storm curtains in place. (Author's collection)

The wooden parts were milled at Ford's Iron Mountain plant in northern Michigan. These pieces were then shipped to the Murray Corporation where assembly took place. The completed wooden bodies were sent to the various Ford plants for final assembly on a chassis.

Ford produced nearly 5000 woody station wagons in 1929, and over 1500 more until production ceased in May, 1930.

Although highly successful, there were problems with the new production wagons. Water leaks were a major complaint, as were minor injuries caused by the sharp lower corners of the wooden doors.

Remedies, though, were quick and easy. Weather stripping or windlace was added to the door sills and jams, while the sharp bottom corners of doors were simply rounded off.

Despite the huge sales success of the Model A, Ford was forced by the innovative competition to offer a fresher, more modern looking Model A for 1930, although mechanically it remained virtually the same.

Soon after the stock market crash in 1929 that heralded the Great Depression, Ford dropped its prices on all of these new Model A Fords, including the station wagon that was reduced to $650.

The interest, and response to, the latest version of Ford's Model A continued to be strong, with nearly four million people witnessing unveilings throughout the US on December 31st.

The newly styled Model A station wagon didn't appear until June 1930, and the price was reduced almost immediately to $640 in these tougher economic times. The new woody wagon would be greeted with equal enthusiasm and, by August 1932, total domestic, Canadian and foreign production would reach 11,881 units.

New car body styles were introduced in the Model

American Woodies

Other car companies offered chassis that could accommodate a custom-built station wagon or sedan delivery. These small wagon- and coachbuilders often fitted less than elegant bodies. Seen here is a rare 1928 Durant Station Wagon. (Author's collection)

A's last year, including another woody. The new 1931 woody was known as the Natural Wood Delivery, fitted with a birch and maple body built by Baker-Raulang. Similar in overall appearance to the station wagon, it featured the usual wooden paneled sides and just two side doors rather than four, but with two other doors in the rear for loading.

The 1931 Natural Wood Delivery, or Type 225-A, was listed at $615, but production totaled a mere 904 examples, including the 19 built in 1930 and the last 40 built in 1932.

Another rarely seen spin-off of this woody was a camper/caravan-like version known as the Travelers' Wagon. It was aimed specifically at the South American market, without wooden side panels but with mosquito netting and roll-down windows.

Both Henry and son, Edsel Ford, had predicted a decade or more of production for the Model A, and sales exceeding the 15 million Model T Fords built. Sales in 1931, due in the most part to the worsening depression, tumbled 50 per cent by December 31st.

Still, Ford did lead the way in station wagon sales, and would continue to dominate the market right into the era of the all-steel versions.

At the same time, competitors were not about to hand over the entire station wagon market to Ford.

American woodies – an emerging market: 1932-1942

Not surprisingly with the Depression deepening by 1932, the number of builders supplying wooden bodies for station wagons had reduced considerably.

York and Hoover had merged, as did Hercules with Campbell – to form the Hercules-Campbell Body Company. Hercules had been a major supplier of station wagon bodies to Chevrolet, so it was no surprise that Hercules-Campbell continued this association with the General Motors division, offering a wide range of wooden bodies, from basic utilitarian to quite stylish and sophisticated. By the middle of the decade a second merger took place, this time with the Waterloo Body Company, to form Mid-State Body, which would build most of Chevrolet's woody station wagons.

Cantrell survived the Depression by building bodies for Chrysler and GM chassis, as well as by diversifying its wood product line.

Some companies built everything from coffins to cabinetry.

By the end of 1932 the large Martin-Parry production facilities had been purchased by Chevrolet. Long-established Mifflinburg still offered a station wagon body, but now focused on supplying cabs, etc, for the trucking industry, before finally closing in 1941.

Joseph Wildanger established the Joseph Wildanger Company in 1922, following years of service building Ford Model T Express and Depot Hack bodies with J H Mount. Wildanger built bodies for Ford chassis, as well as for Chevrolet and Dodge. It is estimated that Wildanger built 500 wooden station wagon bodies from 1922 to 1932, as well as building bodies for all kinds of commercial applications, from vans to hearses.

Wildanger built his woody station wagons with ash, but the panels varied and were made of poplar, plywood, or, even painted metal. A characteristic of Wildanger bodies was ribbing with tapered edges and squared-off ends. The firm is accredited with building one of the first woodies with roll-down windows, on a 1930 Jordan chassis.

Although having to be re-organized in the mid-1930s, Wildanger continued in business long after WWII.

While most of the suppliers had disappeared or merged by the end of the 1930s, one new company emerged and became a prominent builder of wooden bodies. Ionia Manufacturing of Ypsilanti, Michigan, was established by Don Mitchell in 1938, after he bought the bankrupt Ypsilanti Furniture Company. It soon became the key supplier of wooden bodies for Pontiac, Chevrolet, Oldsmobile and Buick.

Ford was truly the only American car company offering a production woody station wagon. In the beginning, the Mengel Company supplied most of the

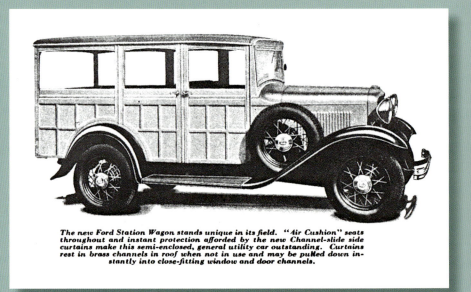

One of the big comfort features on the all-new 1932 Ford Station Wagon was its 'Air Cushion' seats throughout, and instant protection afforded by the new 'Channel-Slide' side and rear curtains. The curtains rested in brass channels in the roof when not in use, and could be instantly pulled down into close-fitting window and door channels. (Author's collection)

The new Ford Station Wagon stands unique in its field. "Air Cushion" seats throughout and instant protection afforded by the new Channel-slide side curtains make this semi-enclosed, general utility car outstanding. Curtains rest in brass channels in roof when not in use and may be pulled down instantly into close-fitting window and door channels.

wooden parts, while Murray, Briggs and Baker-Raulang completed the assembly. However, due to demand which Mengel couldn't handle, in 1934, Ford's own craftsmen began fabricating these parts at the Iron Mountain facility, and shipped these to Murray for assembly.

The maple framing and birch wood was supplied by Ford's own forests. Henry Ford had originally purchased the half-million acres of hardwood forest in Michigan to supply the required wood framing for his Model Ts, but by 1922 had opened his own Iron Mountain sawmills.

Ford introduced the new Flathead V8 in 1932, but not initially for its commercial truck line, of which the station wagon was a part. The 50hp, 4-cylinder engine with its 4.6 to 1 compression ratio remained the standard power unit in the station wagon.

In 1932 Ford built just 334 station wagons, but with the V8 models offered in 1933 that number leapt to 1654; with 2905 in 1934; 5575 in 1935, and 6490 in 1936.

Even by the 1934 model year, only Dodge, Plymouth and Ford listed a station wagon in its commercial

Continued on page 24

American woodies – an emerging market – 1932-1942

The new-for-1933 Ford V8 station wagon was touted for its versatility, and seen as the perfect vehicle for transporting people, baggage or equipment for camping or deliveries. Ford was also beginning to promote its woody wagon as not only being practical, but also "… Unusually smart in appearance." (Author's collection)

www.velocebooks.com
Information on all books • New book news • Special offers • Gift vouchers

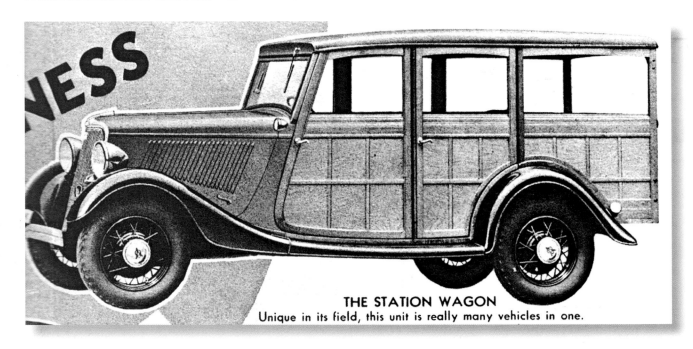

Ford continued to advertise its little-changed 1934 Station Wagon as part of its full truck line and called it "unique in its field ..." It is a passenger car and bus, baggage and equipment carrier, camp car and delivery wagon. It will seat eight, including the driver." The tailgate serves as a luggage rack. (Author's collection)

Combining the facilities of a passenger car with those of a light commercial chassis, and with de luxe passenger appointments, the 7-passenger 1936 Ford station wagon also now featured a tailgate with a compensating spring. With the center and rear seats removed the wagon provided a cargo length of 77in (196cm); a height of 45in (114cm); and width of 52.5in (134cm). (Author's collection)

The 1936 Ford woody station wagon was built on the 112in wheelbase commercial chassis which featured a long list of standard equipment, including glass windows in the front doors. Glass would be fitted throughout in 1937. (Author's collection)

Ford was proud of the fact its sedan delivery and station wagon utilized the same instruments and instrument panel from its passenger cars, and provided the same comfort and detailing (1936). (Author's collection)

Ford's unusual front end styling for 1938 proved less than popular. Even a stylish wooden body did little for the overall look. A major restyle came in 1939. Still, by this time, professional trades people, contractors, photographers and advertising executives bought a woody to enhance their image. (Courtesy Tom McPherson)

catalog. Ford's station wagons would remain part of its commercial line-up through 1937.

By 1936 Ford was building its own station wagons on a production line at Iron Mountain, which allowed for the fabrication of wooden bodies and assembly at one site. Final assembly still required Ford to ship station wagons to fifteen plants across the United States.

Ford station wagons sold even better with production totaling 9430 in 1937; 7218 in 1938; 10,872 in 1939, and 9933 in 1940.

The popularity of the Ford woody wagon stemmed from more than its long history, dependability and solid construction. Ford paid close attention to what its customers wanted, and was constantly offering many new and often very innovative features. For example, in 1939 Ford stressed its new front seat was easily adjustable by up to 4.5 inches (11cm), and the fact the glass lowered into the front doors, while the side glass was sliding and came with locks for better security. Other appreciated features included a tailgate that was fitted with "... a weight compensating spring" to facilitate raising and lowering, and additional interior room and cargo space, thanks in part to Ford having mounted the spare tire on the tailgate. As well, a cover and lock came as standard equipment on the spare.

These sportsmen in 1939 were not mere hunters out for a spot of shooting. Ford saw its Station Wagon as being more for people with a 'station' in life. Note the country house and the chauffeur unloading blankets. This was the De Luxe wagon. (Author's collection)

www.velocebooks.com
Information on all books • New book news • Special offers • Gift vouchers

American Woodies

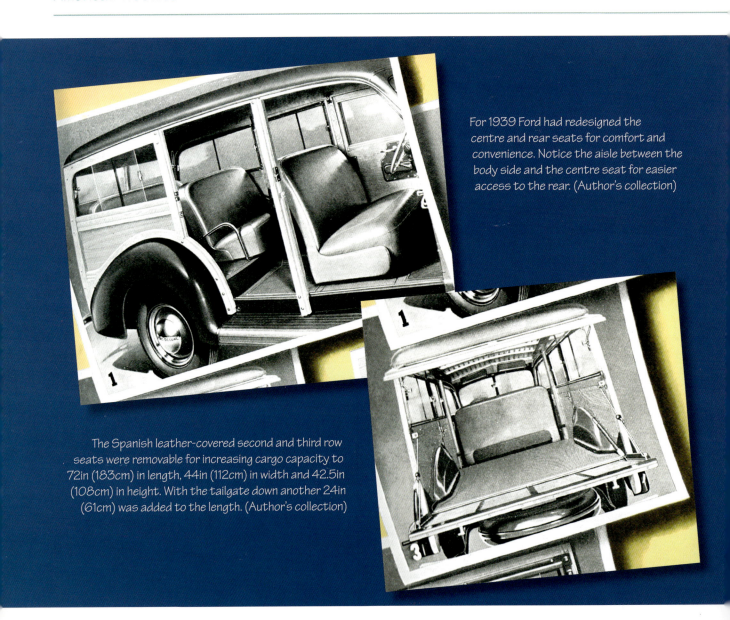

For 1939 Ford had redesigned the centre and rear seats for comfort and convenience. Notice the aisle between the body side and the centre seat for easier access to the rear. (Author's collection)

The Spanish leather-covered second and third row seats were removable for increasing cargo capacity to 72in (183cm) in length, 44in (112cm) in width and 42.5in (108cm) in height. With the tailgate down another 24in (61cm) was added to the length. (Author's collection)

American woodies – an emerging market – 1932-1942

Ford also offered a less expensive Station Wagon in 1939 simply designated the Ford V-8 Station Wagon for what it termed "… the workaday world." Considered users were, "… engineers, surveyors, telephone maintenance and repair crews, scientific expeditions and others." The 'others' we are led to assume were the antique rocking chair collectors! (Author's collection)

This very natural setting, and Ford's latest 1941 woody, was ideal for a press photo. (Courtesy Tom McPherson)

This press photo of a 1942 Mercury shows none of the glamour of high society, country inns or rustic outdoor living despite being the most expensive car offered by the division. Station wagons were also popular as a family vehicle and with proprietors of small businesses. The Mercury station wagon was first introduced in 1941 and 2143 of the maple and birch models were built. In war-shortened 1942 total production was just 857 units. (Courtesy Tom McPherson)

When the 1941 models were introduced America had anticipated entering the war, but carried on introducing new cars for the 1942 model year. This was cut short by the attack on Pearl Harbour, so few of these stylish and distinctive 1942 Fords were built. The 1942 Ford featured doors and a tailgate that could be locked. Safety glass was fitted all around. "The Ford station wagon holds a special place of its own in the American motoring scene." It would be another four years until the next new wagons would appear in showrooms. (Courtesy Tom McPherson)

Ford's upscale Mercury line first appeared in 1939, and soon there were Mercury woody station wagons available for those wanting something a little more exclusive, with all the Ford proven parts.

Chrysler's Dodge and Plymouth Divisions would eventually become Ford's closest competitor in the woody market, but things got off to a slow start.

Both Plymouth and Dodge offered a station wagon in the 1933 catalog. It was supplied by US Body and Forging Company.

In the early thirties under 100 chassis had been sold by Dodge division, but as the market grew by 1934 well

Continued on page 32

American woodies – an emerging market – 1932-1942

For the growing number of outdoorsmen and family campers, many accessories were available to make life easier. This 1937 Dodge Westminster was custom ordered to carry a camping kitchenette that included an icebox, cutlery drawer, stove, oven, and storage for pots, pans and plates.
(Courtesy Christopher Lawrence)

American Woodies

Dodge's fresh styling from 1936 was essentially carried over into 1937, but more importantly, like Ford, Chrysler also offered all glass windows in 1937 in its woody station wagons. The US Body and Forging Company supplied bodies for the Westchester models. This restored example (2006), has been in the Lawrence family since new when it was purchased by the owner's father, famed James Lawrence. He purchased the Dodge in Los Angeles after viewing Clark Gable's Westchester Suburban in his garage. All of the Westchester Suburban wagons were by special order, and the Dodge salesman advised Mr Lawrence that the only vehicle he was aware of in the LA area that he could look at before placing his order was Mr Gable's car. (Courtesy Christopher Lawrence)

American woodies – an emerging market – 1932-1942

A woody station wagon could always be custom-ordered to suit the owner's requirements. Artist and photographer James Lawrence's 1937 Dodge Westchester Suburban was ordered with an extra 30-gallon (114-litre) fuel tank, an extra 6-volt battery, a modified rear bumper, a rear wooden shelf for carrying a camp kitchenette, and special interior cabinetry built above the side and rear windows for storage of art and photographic supplies. (Courtesy Christopher Lawrence)

American Woodies

over 1000 chassis were being built, with many becoming woody station wagons.

By 1938 Dodge was building its own factory Westchester station wagon, but with production totaling just 375 units it was soon dropped. Still, a station wagon was offered in the catalog, and more chassis continued to be delivered and fitted with wagon bodies by various suppliers, but mainly US Body and Forging.

Plymouth, on the other hand, fared slightly better and sold more. This Chrysler Division also sold a production station wagon – again known as the Westchester – in 1938, with sales peaking at 555 units. Yet, in 1939 Plymouth wooden station wagon production increased to 1777 units, and it was now a factory production model. Plymouth production jumped to 3206 in 1940 and 5811 in 1941, before dropping to 1136 in 1942 with America entering the war.

The Dodge D11 Series helped celebrate Dodge's 25th Anniversary with all-new styling. This publicity shot of a 1938 Dodge was taken to prove the usefulness of a woody wagon for inns and lodges. Note minor styling changes such as moving the headlamps to the top of the fenders. (Courtesy Bill Filbert)

This 1938 Dodge Woodie Model RC is a ½-ton (454kg) Commercial with a body by Cantrell. (Courtesy Dale Morse)

American woodies – an emerging market – 1932-1942

Plymouth described its 1939 'Sportsmen' station wagon as an "all-purpose car." For 1939 it was now "roomier", being built on the De Luxe Plymouth chassis. Note the all-natural wood colour and train station setting. (Author's collection)

As well as horsey country settings, something like a dog racing event seemed exclusive enough for the potential buyers of a 1940 Plymouth Sportsmen station wagon. Note how well everyone is dressed, including the dog handlers and racing officials. (Courtesy Tom McPherson)

Chrysler's DeSoto line also began offering a station wagon in its catalog in 1937.

Production of the 1941 Chryslers began in August of that year. An important new entry was the Windsor model-based Town & Country barrelback wagon. Built on the long wheelbase chassis, only 200 of these five-door, six-passenger wagons were produced along with another 797 of the nine-passenger versions of this future classic. Despite its more-sedan-like looks, the 1941 Chrysler T&C was labeled a station wagon. It was an immediate success and would be even more so following WWII.

Chevrolet introduced the first all-steel Carry-All in 1935, also known as the Suburban. (Decades would pass before Chevrolet officially claimed this as a corporate model name.)

Plymouth once again used the Sportsmen name that had been introduced in 1939 when the station wagon model became part of its car model line, rather than a commercial vehicle. This 1941 Sportsmen was built on the 117in (297cm) wheelbase, Special De Luxe Plymouth chassis, and was available with either two-tone or natural finish body. The auxiliary seats were removable and interchangeable. (Author's collection)

American woodies – an emerging market – 1932-1942

This eight-seater was built on a truck chassis and therefore seen more as a two-door commercial vehicle based on Chevrolet's panel truck.

It should be noted, though, that the 1946 Jeep station wagon is considered to be the first all-steel example, although the first truly all-car chassis with an all-steel body was the Plymouth in 1949, but Crosley fans might argue that point.

Although woody station wagons were sold on Chevrolet car and truck chassis, the first Chevrolet's car-based chassis station wagon didn't appear in its truck catalog until 1939, whereas Pontiac promoted a wagon in 1937.

The woody station wagon body was supplied by Ionia, which would be GM's major supplier for its various divisions until the last 1953 Buick woody wagon was built.

Continued on page 38

In March 1941 Chrysler introduced its woody Town and Country models in six and nine passenger 'barrelback' wagon versions. Although it had a steel roof, body framing consisted of white ash with mahogany veneer panels. The name stemmed from a Chrysler-commissioned Boyertown Body Works car, built in 1939 on a Dodge chassis, that the firm dubbed 'Town and Country.' (Courtesy Tom McPherson)

American Woodies

Rather than a tailgate, the new 1941 Town and Country station wagon had clamshell rear wooden doors for loading. Note also the chrome and wooden slat roof rack for additional luggage. On the nine passenger models the rear seat slid back 18in (46cm), and the middle seat cleverly folded out of the front seat. 998 examples were built. (Author's collection)

www.velocebooks.com
Information on all books • New book news • Special offers • Gift vouchers

American woodies – an emerging market – 1932-1942

The 1942 Chrysler Town and Country was again based on the Windsor model. A few changes in outline had taken place, but its barrelback design remained. Around a thousand were built before war curtailed production. (Courtesy Harold Mermel)

American Woodies

As well as the 'Big Three' – Chrysler, Ford and GM – the struggling independent automakers also offered woody station wagons. Needless to say, production totals were very low, but Studebaker, Willys, Packard, and even Bantam, with its Austin Seven-based models, offered a woody wagon.

Studebaker came up with its first factory woody in 1937 fitted with a body supplied by the US Body and Forging Company. Limited production and demand resulted in the station wagon model being dropped with the last of the 1939 models.

Even smaller production makers such as Graham and Hupp supplied chassis for station wagons. The first international woody wagon appeared in 1935, but it was truck-based.

Throughout the 1930s the woody station wagon market continued as a small, yet growing and profitable niche market for the financially healthier car companies.

The woody station wagon was often a showcase model since it was also one of the most expensive offered. In addition, the woody was the most demanding model in regard to maintenance. Yet, despite this, and

Continued on page 42

Chevrolet introduced its all-steel, truck-based, eight-passenger, two-door Carry-All Suburban in 1935. Note that all windows were glass. (Author's collection)

American woodies – an emerging market – 1932-1942

In 1933 Chevrolet didn't offer a woody station wagon in its line-up, but did sell ½-ton chassis as used on its pickup trucks. Pictured is what's believed to be a dealer-arranged woody wagon fitted with a Mifflinburg body built for estate use. The glass side windows were all fixed (the rearmost temporarily enclosed with plywood). (Courtesy W Peters)

American Woodies

The publicity shots (opposite) for this 85hp, six-cylinder, 1940 Chevrolet utilized additional lights inside to show off its interior and well turned-out owners. Chevrolet had introduced a production station wagon again in 1939 and, despite the fact it was priced at $100 less than the comparable Ford woody, it failed to sell in high numbers, with only 989 being built in 1939; 2126 in 1940; 2045 in 1941, and 1057 in the short 1942 model year. (Courtesy Bob Jacoveet & Fred Ruetz)

American woodies – an emerging market – 1932-1942

A leader in the low-priced field in America, Pontiac offered its first production woody Station Wagon in 1937, although not many examples were built. The 1938 Pontiac woody could be ordered with an 85hp six or a 100hp straight-eight engine. (Courtesy Tom McPherson)

Built on the passenger car chassis, this 1939 Pontiac Silver Streak was powered by the latest version of the reliable L-head six-cylinder engine, which promised increased economy that year. (Author's collection)

American Woodies

This factory photo of a 1937 Packard woody station wagon conveyed both the elegance and stature of the car and Packard clientele – and was the most expensive in the new six-cylinder 115 Series. Still, Packard stressed its new lower prices. The woody appeared halfway through 1937, and was fitted with a Cantrell body. (Courtesy Tom McPherson)

By 1939, Pontiac had added a white ash with birch panel body from Ionia to complement the Hercules white ash and mahogany paneled body style initially offered in 1937. (Courtesy Tom McPherson)

The 1941 Packard woody station wagon was available in both Standard and Deluxe trim as a One-Ten or One-Twenty model fitted with a Hercules body. The total number of wagons built in 1941 is estimated to be around 358. (Courtesy Tom McPherson)

the fact that Mifflinburg had built the first all-steel body for a station wagon for a Chevrolet chassis in 1935, automobile-based woody station wagon bodies continued to be offered. It had already become a tradition in North America; an image and an expectation.

The woody station wagon also kept pace with car styling, becoming less square and more rounded. The wooden station wagon bodies complemented the more streamlined, curved lines in automobile design that continued to emerge in the second half of the 1930s.

American woodies – an emerging market – 1932-1942

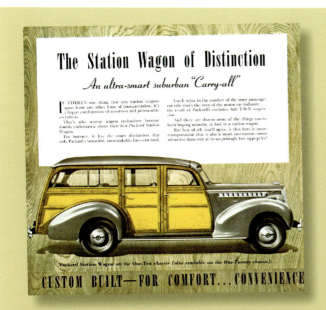

The American Bantam evolved from American Austin, which built cars based on the popular, diminutive British Austin Seven. Production began in 1937, and in 1938 a woody station wagon was added to the line-up. Pictured is a 1938 model. (Courtesy Bill Spear)

The 1940 Packard Station Wagon was available on the One-Ten or larger One-Twenty chassis. Packard played up its smooth ride, as well as the "… happy combination of smartness and pleasurable usefulness" of its station wagon, but also stressed its new lower price. (Courtesy Tom McPherson)

The 1939 through 1941 Bantam woody station wagons differed only slightly in appearance. The bodies were built by the Mifflinburg Body Company. Production of these tiny four-cylinder woodies ended in 1941. Bantam offered two wagons by this time – its woody, and an all-steel wagon known as a Utility Sedan. Bantam is best remembered today as the original designer of the American Jeep. This setting is where an original photograph was taken for advertising the Bantam woody in 1939. (Courtesy Bill Spear)

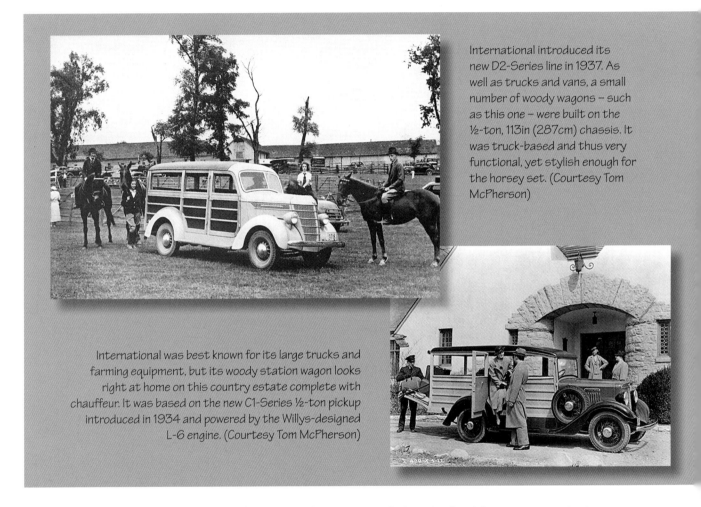

International introduced its new D2-Series line in 1937. As well as trucks and vans, a small number of woody wagons – such as this one – were built on the ½-ton, 113in (287cm) chassis. It was truck-based and thus very functional, yet stylish enough for the horsey set. (Courtesy Tom McPherson)

International was best known for its large trucks and farming equipment, but its woody station wagon looks right at home on this country estate complete with chauffeur. It was based on the new C1-Series ½-ton pickup introduced in 1934 and powered by the Willys-designed L-6 engine. (Courtesy Tom McPherson)

The larger, all-steel and woody truck chassis Suburban models were far too utilitarian in looks and comfort, and lacked the styling forte of a woody station wagon. The Carry-Alls were closer to small buses, and most often provided seating for eight passengers, plus luggage.

At the same time, a woody station wagon made a strong statement about its owners and their status, as well as being a practical hauler of people and goods.

For 1940, International introduced its new K-Series that would continue in production to the end of 1949. The rarely seen woody was just one of 42 models offered on 142 different wheelbases. The woody wagon was built on the light-duty, ½-ton K1 chassis. Pictured is a pre-war K1. (Courtesy Tom McPherson)

This circa 1935 International C-Series woody is very similar in appearance to the 1934 model, but is fitted with smaller wire wheels. (Courtesy Tom McPherson)

During the 1930s Depression, those who could afford the best Duesenberg, Pierce-Arrow or Cadillac would more often prefer to be seen in a less ostentatious automobile. The woody station wagon allowed film stars – especially those who had a connection to the popular western cowboy and Indian genre – the rich, and celebrities from all walks of life, to 'dress down' while still being fashionable and attract attention whenever they wanted it.

Every manufacturer building wooden station wagon bodies used similar construction methods, but strove to create its own unique style. This was accomplished via the colour of contrasting wood stains; the mixture of horizontal and vertical strapping and framing; the subtle shaping and lines that made each one distinctive, along with certain styling cues in each design.

For example, Ford had a distinguishing arrangement of vertical and horizontal ribbing, while Cantrell used its own combination of ribbing arrangements, and US Body and Forging was noted

Continued on page 48

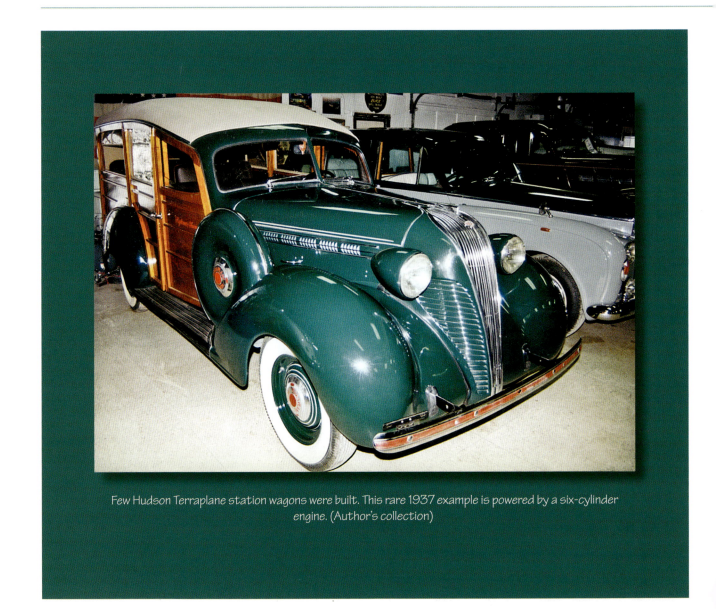

Few Hudson Terraplane station wagons were built. This rare 1937 example is powered by a six-cylinder engine. (Author's collection)

American woodies – an emerging market – 1932-1942

Hudson offered this stylish woody station wagon in 1939. Fender skirts, wide whitewall tires, bumper guards, a radio, driving lights and a spotlight all add to its pizzazz. (Author's collection)

No Cadillac production station wagons were ever built, so it was left to Buick to come up with a flagship. Buick did this admirably, as seen in this 1940 example. Its styling and solid construction resulted in the Buick becoming one of the most popular Woodies in America. (Courtesy Tom McPherson)

While Oldsmobile held virtually the same status as Buick in General Motors, it lacked the overall styling flare as demonstrated by this 1940 woody station wagon. Based on the 70-Series, the wagon came in both Standard and DeLuxe trim. (Courtesy Tom McPherson)

for its simple, uncluttered designs and the distinctive red gum wood used in the beltline of its Dodge and Plymouth station wagon bodies.

By the mid 1930s more wooden custom-bodied sedans and convertibles were beginning to appear, built as special orders. These very stylish, attention-getting models soon caught the eye of Chrysler and Ford, both of which went on to develop production models.

Throughout the 1930s many custom woodies were built by a multitude of companies, some larger and better known, whilst others fabricated one-off, very professional-looking designs.

As the decade was ending, more and more 4x4 woody station wagons were appearing. Marmon-Herrington began offering Ford conversions in 1937, and these were among the most popular.

American woodies – an emerging market – 1932-1942

Here's a special order eight door, 1940 LaSalle woody station wagon built by Meteor for Matilda Dodge-Wilson – the Dodge Bros heiress. The Wilsons apparently used the LaSalle on their Meadow Brook estate to transport servants to Detroit on their day off, or to carry the local sports team to games. Professional car builder Meteor seemingly built a few other woody station wagons over its long history.
(Courtesy Tom McPherson)

Very rarely seen was a 1940 Willys woody four-door station wagon. Willys woody station wagons were fitted with bodies supplied by US Body and Forging Company. Willys made only a minute number of woody wagons between the last half of the 1930s and into the 1940s. For example, only five are thought to have been built in 1940.
(Courtesy Tom McPherson)

The 1942 121in wheelbase Buick Special Model 49 came equipped with a Fireball straight-eight engine. Advertising made special mention of the front door armrests. (Courtesy Tom McPherson)

American woodies – the finest and last: 1945-1953

Along with all the havoc and destruction, WWII brought great innovation in airplane and vehicle manufacture. The lessons learnt could now be applied to peacetime production. As a result, the post-war years saw many changes in automobile design and construction.

The post-war automobile market was huge due to a pent-up consumer demand for new vehicles. The American public needed new cars, and many small businesses required vehicles in order to continue operating as well. At the same time, new, emerging businesses accompanied the boom in housing, suburban expansion, highway and commercial construction.

In peacetime North America, in areas where there had not been large-scale destruction of ports and cities, families could now think about using their new leisure time to see the USA. A new car was needed to go on trips, go camping, or holiday at lodges and resorts.

Ford for 1946 declared its Sportsman was, "Smarter than Smart!" Features of the stylish 1946 Ford Sportsman included a new 100hp, V8 engine, new oversized, self-centering hydraulic brakes with 12in (30.5cm) drums, six-passenger leather seats and a trunk large enough to carry plenty of luggage. (Author's collection)

American woodies – the finest and last: 1945-1953

Despite the fact that 1946 production line Ford models were more or less a carry-over in design, the company declared that the latest Sportsman model was "Something really new!" (Author's collection)

When the 1946 models finally began coming off the assembly lines, American car manufacturers were concentrating on turning out sedans and trucks. The automobile manufacturers rushed mildly face-lifted model ranges into production, with new model names introduced to add freshness and aid differentiation, as did the few mechanical changes implemented.

The still niche market woody station wagon was not a major concern to the surviving independents at this point, yet was still part of the 'Big Three's' line-up in 1946.

Ford was ready to meet the post-war demand for new cars, and built its first cars by the end of 1945. By that time, Henry Ford II had already delivered a Ford and Mercury convertible to Iron Mountain to convert to a woody, and compete with Chrysler's prestigious T&C line. The sheet metal was removed, a superstructure built, and ash and mahogany applied.

Features of the stylish 1946 Ford Sportsman included a new 100hp, V8 engine, new oversized, self-centering, hydraulic brakes with 12in (18cm) drums, six leather passenger seats and a trunk large enough to carry plenty of luggage.

American Woodies

Although the Ford Motor Company was struggling after the war, it was aggressively seeking sales. One of its 1946 top-of-the-line models was its stylish woody Sportsman convertible. It was promoted as "Two cars in one ... Ford designers have combined the paneled smartness of the station wagon and the touch-a-button convenience of the convertible!" (Author's collection)

The 1946 Ford Sportsman featured a convertible top that, by pushing a button, could be raised or lowered in just 30 seconds. That didn't, of course, include releasing or securing the snaps on the cloth boot. (Author's collection)

The 1946 Ford Station Wagon was offered in DeLuxe or Super DeLuxe models. Few changes were made from 1946-1948, and the 1948 model would be the last of the traditional Ford woodies. Still, in that shortened production year, approximately 8900 Super DeLuxe station wagons were built. (Courtesy Tom McPherson)

Ford offered its Sportsman Ford models in 1946 through 1948, but the Mercury version was dropped after the first year after only 200 Sportsman convertibles were made. Sportsman sales amounted to 723 in 1946; 2774 in 1947, and just 28 in 1948.

Meanwhile, Ford woody station wagons resumed immediate production and remained virtually unchanged from 1946 to 1948. Total Ford woody wagon sales in 1946 reached a whopping 16,960 with 16,104 units in 1947, before dropping to about half that number in 1947.

American Woodies

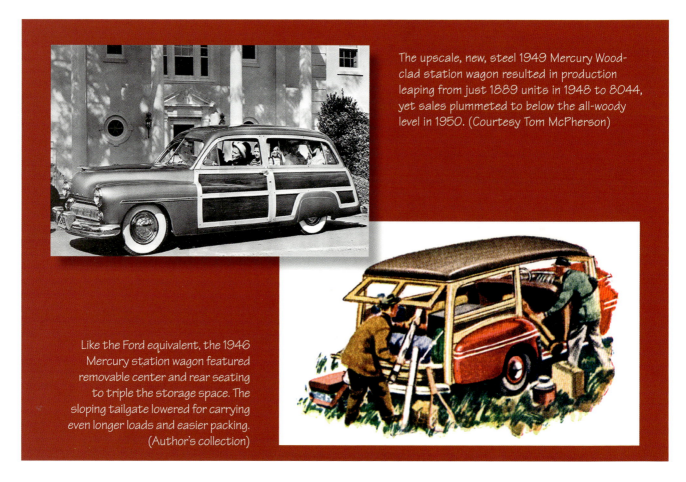

The upscale, new, steel 1949 Mercury Wood-clad station wagon resulted in production leaping from just 1889 units in 1948 to 8044, yet sales plummeted to below the all-woody level in 1950. (Courtesy Tom McPherson)

Like the Ford equivalent, the 1946 Mercury station wagon featured removable center and rear seating to triple the storage space. The sloping tailgate lowered for carrying even longer loads and easier packing. (Author's collection)

Over at Mercury, sales from 1946 to 1948 were 2767, 3558 and 1889 units respectively.

Ford introduced its first all-new car in 1949, and its new two-door wagon was well publicized. Ford wagon sales rocketed to 31,412 units in 1949 before dropping to 22,929 in 1950 as the entire market slumped. By the time the last real woody wagons came off the assembly line in 1951, that figure had rebounded to 29,017.

In 1952, with the newly styled, all-steel wagon and three model ranges, sales more than doubled. The Country Squire - with its simulated mahogany panels

Continued on page 58

For those wanting a slightly nicer trim level on their Ford station wagon there was the Mercury eight-passenger model. (Author's Collection)

The 1946 Mercury had all the Ford features, plus more. The leather interior came in a choice of colours: tan; red or grey. (Author's collection)

The 1946 Mercury's custom-built looks were the result of maple body framing combined with a choice of rich birch or deep-toned mahogany panels. Note this Canadian version had different styling. (Courtesy Tom McPherson)

The '49 Ford has been awarded the Fashion Academy Gold Medal as the 'Fashion Car of the Year'

For 1949 Ford referred to its latest eight-passenger hauler as its new "Dream Wagon." Ford went with just two doors rather than four, but despite its attempt at convincing the public this was better than four narrow doors, provided greater visibility and was "… a blessing to parents of small children" the company would later bring back the more convenient four-door wagon version. (Author's collection)

For 1949, Ford station wagons were all steel construction although real wood trim and plywood paneling were added even to the rear tailgate. Perhaps an owner kneeling on the roof and banging his fist on the steel roof panel was going a bit overboard to prove a point. (Author's collection)

American woodies – the finest and last: 1945-1953

Ford had always prided itself on its styling, and the all-new 1949 models – including the new station wagons – won all sorts of accolades. The wagon was awarded the 'Fashion Academy Gold Medal' as 'Fashion Car of the Year.' (Author's collection)

For 1947 Mercury woody station wagon sales continued to climb from 2797 units to 3558. (Courtesy Tom McPherson)

This 1950 Ford woody station wagon advertisement promoted a new family lifestyle in the great outdoors. (Courtesy Tom McPherson)

American Woodies

Ford had introduced its Country Squire, a soon to be iconic nameplate, in 1950. Although these 1951 Country Squire two-door wagons were of all-steel construction, real wood still adorned the sides and rear tailgate. Officially the last Ford woody, a 1951 Country Squire, left Iron Mountain on December 5, 1951. (Courtesy Tom McPherson)

1952 was the last year that real wood was used on a Ford Motor Company vehicle. The Crestline County Squire featured this, and apparently a few 1953 Mercury models left the factory with wood trim. All-steel meant less maintenance for the ever increasing number of station wagon owners. (Tom McPherson Collection)

and just minimal wood framing found 5429 buyers. That number would nearly double the following year, and in 1954 peak at 12,797. Yet, by 1954 there was no real wood trim on Ford station wagons and, understandably, Mercury as well.

The similar up-market Mercury version sold in substantially smaller numbers compared to the Ford in 1949, (8044 units), but fared well when measured against its direct competitors.

Sales would drop to just over 1700 wagons in 1950, before rebounding slightly to 3812 in 1951. Fresh Mercury styling in 1952 helped, but not until full production of the all-steel, minimal real wood trim 1954 Mercury station wagon did sales begin to climb steadily and surpass the 1949 figure.

Chrysler, in the early post-war years, offered the widest range of woodies. While its T&C sedan and convertible were virtually unchanged in 1946, it had

custom deluxe station wagon

Here's new Meteor beauty combined with practical utility... the Meteor "Country Squire" Station Wagon, a town and country car! There's room for eight in comfort and it converts to a "carry-all" easily. Just lift out rear seat, fold down middle seat and there's 38.8 sq. ft. of level cargo space with tailgate lowered. Beautiful interiors are panelled in mahogany with Golden Tan and Brown Vinyl trim. Baked-on enamel body colours are standard with exterior panelling of selected hardwood backed with steel for added safety. Special Station Wagon structural strengthening plus big 60-inch rear treads provide for half-ton loads.

Here's a Canadian version from Ford known as a 1951 Meteor Custom DeLuxe Station Wagon. In 1949 the Meteor nameplate was introduced in Canada. It was basically a low price Mercury clothed with a Ford body and powered by the familiar Flathead V8. In 1950 the wagon was added to the Custom DeLuxe line-up. For 1951 Meteor got its own distinctive, non-Mercury grille. (Courtesy Tom McPherson)

Following WWII, Chrysler re-introduced its popular and prestigious woody car line-up. This is a 1946 Chrysler Town and Country two-door convertible powered by a 325.5in^3 (5.3-litre) straight-eight. (Courtesy Walt McCall)

www.velocebooks.com
Information on all books • New book news • Special offers • Gift vouchers

American woodies – the finest and last: 1945-1953

"WOODIES" of the past included one of the first, a 1941 Chrysler Town and Country (top) and a Chrysler Town and Country which was popular in the 1946-48 era.

From: Chrysler-Plymouth Public Relations, P.O. 1919, Detroit, MI 48288 (82-532)

CHRYSLER-PLYMOUTH NEWS PHOTO

hoped to expand the line-up to include a roadster, two-door hardtop and Brougham. The T&C models were, depending on the model, built on both the 127in (323cm) New Yorker with a straight-eight engine, and the smaller 122in (310cm) Windsor chassis with a six-cylinder engine. As production began late, in October, few T&C models were built in 1946.

While Dodge did not have a production station wagon until 1949, Plymouth introduced its mildly changed pre-war design in 1946. Cantrell and others did build some Dodge Woodies on the light truck chassis, but in very small numbers.

As well as convertible and sedan Town and Country models, in 1946 Chrysler also introduced a stylish two-door hardtop, but only seven were built and this Town and Country body style was dropped and did not reappear until 1950. The limited production 1946 two-door hardtop Town and Country has the distinction of being the first built by any American manufacturer following WWII. (Courtesy Walt McCall)

American Woodies

There were few changes in the appearance of the 1946-1948 Chrysler Town and Country models. (1947 example pictured courtesy Paul Jenkins)

For those looking to haul lots of baggage, yet wanting the comfort of a four-door sedan, Chrysler offered an optional full roof luggage rack on its Town and Country sedan, in addition to its cavernous trunk. (1947 example pictured courtesy Paul Jenkins)

In 1948 Chrysler built 3309 of its 323in^3 (5.3L) straight-eight Town and Country convertibles such as this fine example seen in the company's museum in Auburn Hills, Michigan. (Author's collection)

American woodies – the finest and last: 1945-1953

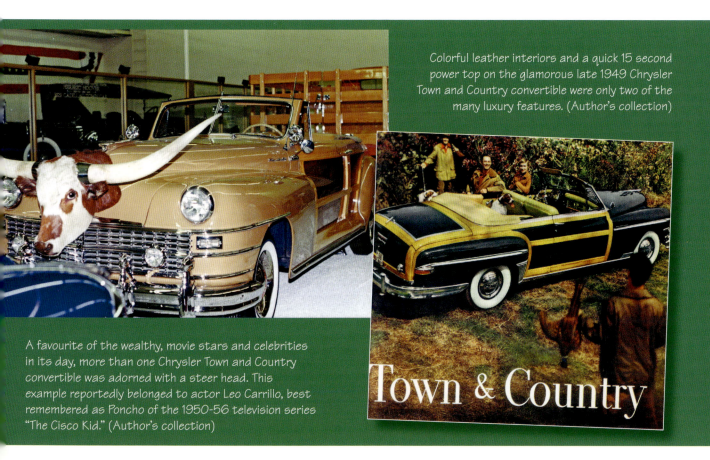

Colorful leather interiors and a quick 15 second power top on the glamorous late 1949 Chrysler Town and Country convertible were only two of the many luxury features. (Author's collection)

A favourite of the wealthy, movie stars and celebrities in its day, more than one Chrysler Town and Country convertible was adorned with a steer head. This example reportedly belonged to actor Leo Carrillo, best remembered as Poncho of the 1950-56 television series "The Cisco Kid." (Author's collection)

Chrysler dropped its T&C woody sedan in 1948 as production fell to 1176 units, and for 1949 the Royal woody station wagon joined the still popular convertible. With costs ever increasing, and convertible production down nearly a third to just 1375 examples, it was replaced in 1950 with a new and very stylish 2-door hardtop. Yet, with just 701 hardtops and 600 Royal woody station wagons finding owners, the writing was on the wall. Chrysler's reputation had been greatly enhanced by the T&C models, and such memorable models meant the name would be revived in the future, though the line would never be as grandiose as the original.

Like GM and Ford, Chrysler had introduced all-new models, and those woody wagons built had less wood

Continued on page 67

American Woodies

For the first time, in 1950 Chrysler offered its woody line-up as an all-steel structure except for the polished white ash trim. Wood trim encircled the rear of the car as well as the sides. The newest – and now only – model in the Town and Country line was a stylish two-door hardtop. Although the Town and Country name still appeared in advertising, the model, by 1950, was part of the all-new Chrysler Newport line-up. (Author's collection)

For 1949 the Town and Country sedan was dropped and the station wagon re-introduced. The freshly-styled new Chrysler had Town and Country heritage, but was called the Royal Station Wagon, and helped to celebrate the company's 25th anniversary. Its construction was white ash with mahogany Di-Noc insert panels. (Author's collection)

American woodies – the finest and last: 1945-1953

The Chrysler Royal woody station wagon featured a longer wheelbase, stretched by 4in (10cm). The rear-mounted spare on the Royal was only available in 1949. (Author's collection)

DeSoto began 1950 by offering an S-14 woody station wagon in DeLuxe and Custom trim, but before the model year was out an all-steel version had joined the line-up. (Courtesy Scott and Damian Melcer)

American woodies – the finest and last: 1945-1953

and more steel. It was in 1949 that Plymouth had two wagons. The Special DeLuxe was a four-door woody station wagon with a steel roof, while the DeLuxe was an all-steel, two-door wagon. Dodge and DeSoto only had a woody station wagon in 1949, and by 1950 there were even some Chrysler T&C (99 built and mostly ambulances) all-steel wagons. By 1951 Chrysler was no longer building woodies.

In 1946 Chevrolet introduced its new $1712 Fleetmaster woody station wagon, its most expensive model, yet the 804 examples soon sold. Although very similar in appearance to the previous year, in 1947

Continued on page 73

Chrysler also offered a DeSoto woody wagon in its 1949 line-up. Those buyers looking to move up from a Dodge had a full line-up of more expensive DeSotos to choose from. (Courtesy Bill Filbert)

For 1949 Dodge emphasized its four large doors – as opposed to Ford's two-door wagon. Dodge also noted that the second row seat folded for easier access to the rear seat. There was "… no need to squirm or crawl." (Author's collection)

The '49 Dodge featured a two-piece tailgate. The two rear seats were removable, and the spare was mounted on the tailgate in a locked metal case. (Author's collection)

The new 1949 Dodge Coronet station wagon was described in ads as "… a load-lugging giant." The 'Gyromatic' automatic transmission was optional on this nine-passenger wagon. (Author's collection)

American woodies – the finest and last: 1945-1953

1950 brought all-new styling, but was the last year for Chrysler, Plymouth and Dodge woody station wagons. It's believed only 600 of these Dodge Coronet wagons were produced, and less than a dozen exist today. (Courtesy Jack Huiberts)

American Woodies

PLYMOUTH

IT GOES TO THE STADIUM... FOR EIGHT! This great new Plymouth Station Wagon sets new standards for beauty, utility and long life. Comfortably seats eight full-sized passengers. Both rear seats quickly and easily removed for maximum loading space. Handsome, easy-to-clean vinyl plastic seats and seat backs. Natural-finish bonded plywood body panels with long-life finish on all-wood surfaces. New body construction—new steel floor and top—make this the safest, most rugged Plymouth Station Wagon ever built—with Plymouth engineering throughout. Before you buy—compare!

THE CAR THAT LIKES TO BE COMPARED!

This 1949 Plymouth featured the space-saving continental tire kit which was also seen on the 1949 Dodge woodies. Note the special bumper. (Author's collection)

Although there was no denying the Plymouth Suburban station wagon was far more practical, the beauty and style of the Special De Luxe was hard to resist. The floor and roof only were all-steel. (Author's collection)

Only subtle grille and tail light design changes were evident on the 1950 Plymouth. Two station wagons were offered – the all-steel Suburban and the Special De Luxe Station wagon. (Author's collection)

American Woodies

This 1947 Chevrolet Suburban woody was built on a ½-ton, 116in wheelbase Carry All and pickup chassis, and powered by a 216in^3 (3.5L), 90hp, six-cylinder engine. Cantrell was the builder and its special order woody bodies were actually available through to 1955 for GMC, Chevrolet and Dodge truck chassis. (Courtesy Don Bryant)

American woodies – the finest and last: 1945-1953

For 1947 Chevrolet targeted its woody wagon at the upper middle class family man in America. Sales reached a healthy 4912 units – good for a woody, but by far the lowest production total of the entire Chevy line-up. The woody was also the most expensive Chevrolet model in the Fleetmaster line-up at $1892. (Courtesy Tom McPherson)

The 1949 Chevrolet went from wood to all steel at mid-year, although each sold for a hefty $2267. Both wagons were offered in the Styleline DeLuxe range only. (Courtesy Tom McPherson)

Note the difference in the real wood body on this 1949 Chevrolet compared to the other all-steel version. The rear fender wood is very angular compared to the all-steel, faux-woody production model that was rounded. (Courtesy Tom McPherson)

Chevrolet's woody station wagon of ash and mahogany sported bodies by Fisher as well as Ionia, and production rose to 4912 units.

In the last pre-war styling year of its most expensive model, the 1948 $2013 woody station wagon Chevrolet saw sales more than double to 10,171 units.

1949 heralded the first all-new Chevy since before the war. Fresh styling included two new station wagons.

From a distance the two looked identical, but only the Ionia model featured real wood. The easier-to-maintain, less expensive, all-steel station wagon with the wooden mahogany door and trim panels won out. Production of the last real Chevrolet woody station wagon ceased in mid-year.

Yet, from 1950, Chevy continued to offer a very woody-like, all-steel station wagon.

American Woodies

This 1948 Chevrolet Fleetmaster is fitted with a dealer-installed Fulton Sun Shield. The Fleetmaster broke all previous production records, finding 10,171 buyers in 1948, despite being priced at over $2000 and being a carryover model from 1947. It did have plenty of style, though! (Courtesy Henri David Jr)

American woodies – the finest and last: 1945-1953

Due to the popularity of Chrysler's T&C models and Ford's Sportsman cars, aftermarket companies offered a woody Chevrolet Country Club kit for Chevrolet convertible and Aero sedan owners. However, there were few takers, despite the cost being just $150, plus installation. Other companies offered similar kits for other models, but despite the eye-catching appeal of a woody, it found only a small market and failed to garner much enthusiasm.

By 1951 Chevrolet, GM's largest division, had moved from a woody to a station wagon featuring all-steel construction. Chevy's Styleline DeLuxe station wagon combined the "… smartness and distinction of a woodgrained finish with the strength and safety of an all-steel body." The four-door, eight-passenger 1951 Chevrolet wagon was also plugged for its quieter ride and greater durability. It was noted that the rear seats could be readily removed when extra haulage space was required. (Author's collection)

As the woody era came to a close in the early 1950s, American companies such as Chevrolet offered all-steel station wagons with or without the woody look. This magnificent 1951 all-steel body woody was fully restored, and the wide variety of painted woodgrains inside and out carefully matched to original factory finishes. Adding a woodgrain finish is not an easy task, but can be accomplished by a patient owner such as Brownie Petersen; the results can be spectacular. (Courtesy Edwin L 'Brownie' Petersen)

THE STYLELINE DE LUXE STATION WAGON

Although many design and technical advances were made during WWII, woodie station wagons were built in the traditional pre-war manner as exemplified in this interior shot of a 1946 Pontiac. Note: When restored, the owner added a fitted carpet to protect the new wooden floor. (Courtesy Andrew Mort)

There was a lot of white ash and mahogany in this rare 1946 Pontiac Streamliner DeLuxe Woodie. (Courtesy Andrew Mort)

American Woodies

Pontiac was a slightly up-market version of Chevrolet, and for 1947 carried on building its warmed-over pre-war designs, including two station wagons in its two series; Torpedoes and Streamliners. This top-of-the-line wooden Streamliner wagon was one of ten body styles offered that year. (Courtesy Albert and Kathryn Golden)

American Woodies – the finest and last Woodies – 1945-1953

The Streamliner models were the largest Pontiacs, and featured a 122in (310cm) wheelbase with an overall length of 210in (533cm). The Standard 1948 Streamliner had removable rear seats and rich tan imitation leather upholstery, while the De Luxe offered genuine red leather and wool cloth. Wagons were not available in Canada in either of the lesser Fleetleader or Torpedo lines. (Author's collection)

Pontiac likewise offered pre-war-based woody station wagons starting in 1946 with no real changes. These were very stylish six- and eight-passenger woodies, part of the Streamliner line that continued to be offered basically unchanged through 1948, powered by six- or eight-cylinder engines. Like Chevy, Pontiac featured all-new body styles in 1949, including its woody station wagon. Pontiac followed the same corporate path as Chevy in regard its switchover to all-steel station wagon bodies.

Oldsmobile introduced a very pre-war-looking 1946 woody station wagon, with bodies from either Ionia or Hercules. Just 140 were built of these 66-Series Oldsmobile Woodies which cost $1795. Few changes were made in 1947, except for the price, which rose to $2175, yet more were sold with production hitting 968 units.

Oldsmobile had a new look a year earlier than the other divisions, and that included two woody station wagons. The dramatic-looking 1948 Oldsmobile station wagon was the most expensive in the division's line-up at $2672. Still, 1314 were sold.

In 1949 Oldsmobile offered four different Fisher body station wagon models; two each in its 76 and 88

American Woodies

American woodies – the finest and last: 1945-1953

lines. The woody was basically all-steel except for the trim and tailgate. At $3120, the woody station wagon was the most expensive Oldsmobile, higher priced than any top-of-the-line 98 model. A mere 1355 of this last real woody Oldsmobile were sold. In 1950 Oldsmobile offered its station wagon models again with a minor woody-look, but poor sales resulted in the station wagon being dropped from the Oldsmobile line-up altogether in 1951. Oldsmobile would not re-enter the station wagon market again until 1957.

Buick offered its 1946 woody station wagon as part of the Super series with just 798 built and retailing at $2594, but in 1947 added yet another even more expensive woody station wagon – the Ionia-built Roadmaster, priced at $3249. Total production for both models was around 1000 units.

In 1948, Roadmaster production jumped to well over 2000 units, amidst great anticipation for the all-new 1949 models, and sales edged closer to 3000 of these stylish woody station wagons.

For 1950 and 1951 that production level was maintained, but dropped to 2000 units in 1952. The new, easier to maintain, all-steel wagons were catching on and in the final year of the last real woody production, station wagon sales amounted to just 1830 Ionia built Super 59-Series wagons, and 670 Roadmaster Woodies. It was the end of an era.

Packard introduced a wood-clad station wagon in

Continued on page 87

Left: Only 140 of the 1946 Special 66, eight-seater Oldsmobile Hercules-bodied woody station wagons were built, and this sole surviving example has been in the same family since new. Tom Jeffris' nicely optioned Oldsmobile originally sold for $2297 and came equipped with a four speed, Hydra-Matic transmission, whitewall tires, deluxe steering wheel, push-button radio, electric clock, Condition-Air, heater and defroster. (Courtesy Tom Jeffris & Tim Sheriden)

This Series 66, eight-passenger 1948 Oldsmobile advertisement focused on carrying larger loads rather than people, with a load capacity of 1000lbs. Oldsmobile was the first division to receive the new 'Furturamic' body design, also offered as an 88 model as well. With its steel roof, real wood was just side trim and used on the tailgate. (Courtesy Tom McPherson)

American Woodies

For 1949 Buick offered all-new styling based on GM's C-Body. The Super models had a 121in (305cm) wheelbase as opposed to the Roadmaster 126in (320cm). The woody station wagons were very similar in styling, but the Super 50-Series had three Ventiports on its front fender, while a Roadmaster 70-Series had four. (Courtesy Pete Phillips)

American woodies – the finest and last: 1945-1953

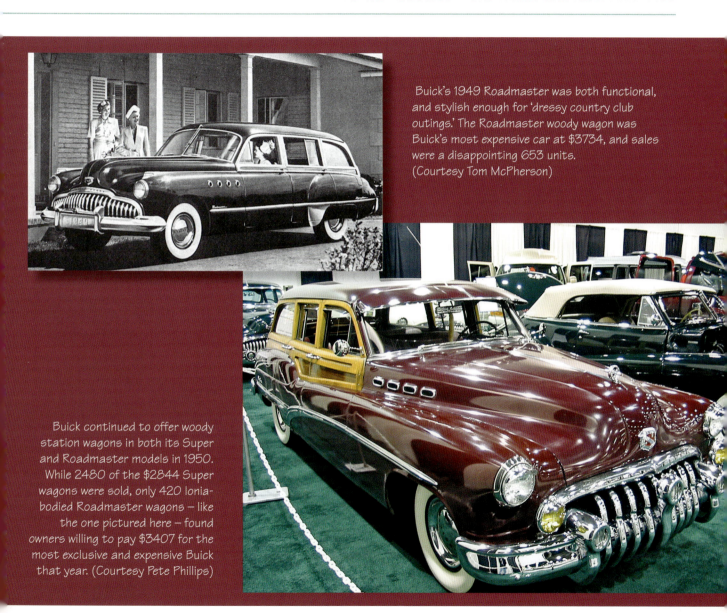

Buick's 1949 Roadmaster was both functional, and stylish enough for 'dressy country club outings.' The Roadmaster woody wagon was Buick's most expensive car at $3734, and sales were a disappointing 653 units. (Courtesy Tom McPherson)

Buick continued to offer woody station wagons in both its Super and Roadmaster models in 1950. While 2480 of the $2844 Super wagons were sold, only 420 Ionia-bodied Roadmaster wagons – like the one pictured here – found owners willing to pay $3407 for the most exclusive and expensive Buick that year. (Courtesy Pete Phillips)

American Woodies

Buick offered its final 1953 Ionia woody wagons in both Super 50 (1830 units) and Roadmaster 70-Series lines (670 units). Although a small number of other woody carry-alls were built after 1953, these very stylish Buicks are considered the last woody production station wagons. It was the end of an era. (Courtesy Pete Phillips)

For 1953 Buick offered a Model 50-Series Super with three port holes rather than four. This is the less expensive 1953 Model 79 Super. (Courtesy Pete Phillips)

American Woodies

Packard offered its woody Station Sedan in 1948, noting its six-passenger luxury, plus easy-loading, carry-all ability. It was all steel with northern birch trim. (Author's collection)

Nash built very few woodies, but by 1947 had introduced this Ambassador Suburban. The basic sedan model was recreated using ash framing and mahogany panels. Like all woodies it was expensive. and even in these post-war boom years only around 1000 were sold from 1946-1948. (Courtesy Tom McPherson)

Over its three year production period from 1948-1950, the Packard Station Sedan was part of the Standard Eight-series and therefore fitted with the smaller 145hp straight-eight. Weighing in at 4075lb (1848kg), it cost the stately sum of $3450.00. (Author's collection)

Crosley built a small number of woody station wagons before the war, but its post-war production models were all-steel, like this 1949 example with a Mylar woodgrain insert. (Courtesy Tom McPherson)

American woodies – the finest and last: 1945-1953

Studebaker had never been a serious competitor in the woody station wagon market before the war. This stylized 1946 Studebaker Champion station wagon was perhaps one of two prototypes, or a one-off special order. The prototypes were rejected as possible production models, and Studebaker did not enter the station wagon market again until 1955. (Courtesy Tom McPherson)

1948 within its all-new model line. It was the first station wagon to be offered by Packard since 1941. It was adorned with northern birch trim and painted woodgrain panels; neither of which were structural, but rather decoration on the steel body. Known as the Packard Standard Station Sedan, it was part of the Standard Eight series and fitted with the smaller straight-eight. By the end of 1950, production ceased after an estimated 3864 had been delivered.

Nash offered a T&C-like Suburban sedan in 1946, but sales were limited; by the end of the 1948 model year only a thousand units had been built.

International built a few woody wagons, as did other very small, post-war manufacturers such as the little-known Keller and Playboy. Meanwhile, post-war models from Jeep and Crosley were given the woody look on an all-steel station wagon body.

Following WWII it had become apparent that all-steel wagons were the future in America. People were beginning to have more free time, new roads and highways were opening regularly, and young families were moving to the suburbs. Also, camping and the outdoor life was the big trend in the American lifestyle.

Even with the reduced amount of real wood in many of the 1949 station wagon models, some substantial additional maintenance was still required. For example, even in the 1949-1951 Ford and Mercury wagons, owners were instructed by the manual to varnish the wood paneling at least once a year, and in areas with seasonal changes, twice a year.

Those companies that had supplied woody bodies had adapted to the loss of business and changeover to all-steel station wagons by merging with other companies, expanding into different wood-based markets, or focusing on existing manufacturing. Still, there were some who were forced to sell out or close down.

Woodies today

Today, in the collector car market, American woodies are highly prized, and therefore carry on the trend of being highly priced in comparison to other body styles. The maintenance of any of these vehicles has been compared to that of a wooden boat. Still, these wooden cars and station wagons have a huge following, with dedicated clubs and enthusiastic owners – many of whom have kindly supplied photographs for this book.

Despite the last real woody being built in 1953, North Americans were, and still are, attracted to the woody-look nearly sixty years later.

Throughout the 1950s and into the 1990s, American automakers offered woody-look station wagons in response to consumer demand, and even in these most modern times DaimlerChrysler offered a woody PT Cruiser in its line-up.

Some enthusiasts like to add the woody look to their cars. Crosley never made a real woody in the 1950s, but, if it had, this interpretation by an enthusiast wouldn't be far off. (Courtesy Tom McPherson)

Very few 1936 Chevrolet woody wagons were built and only a miniscule number survive today. This 'phantom' Chevrolet woody station wagon was built in 2005. Although not an original example it was patterned after an original Campbell body design, with the exception of having two doors rather than four. (Courtesy Carl Stoutenberg)

Woodies today

Over the years, some old car enthusiasts have built wooden bodies on vehicles where the original steel body of a coupe or sedan was far too rusty to be restored. It is a growing trend today.

These more recently constructed woodies are built with the same care and skill as the originals. Most were constructed on the chassis of pre-1940 models, but even post-war cars have sometimes been given the woody treatment for added pizzazz.

Customizers and hot-rodders have also often gone for the woody look over the past sixty years.

So appreciated is the natural wood appearance and feel of real wood, that even more modern vehicles from Jeeps to Cadillacs are being given a woody makeover by North American car enthusiasts.

The woody look has been an endearing styling cue on this continent, whereas in other parts of the world the woody was relegated to the pre-war and early post-war eras. Perhaps it was because European car makers tended to use wood more out of necessity, for floors and convertible top header pieces right into the 1960s, and regard it today as up-market trim and facia treatments, whereas North Americans see the woody look along the flanks of their cars and station wagons as more of an 'ingrained' part of their automotive heritage ...

This custom woody was crafted after a concept drawing by Tom Daniel that appeared on the cover of *Rod & Custom* magazine in June, 1965. (Author's collection)

Not all customs have modern interpretations. This 1940 Ford appears to be almost stock, but features a custom-built frame, completely modern drivetrain, and fiberglass fenders and front end. The wood is real though! (Author's collection)

The wood-look remains popular today, and often enthusiasts go to great lengths to recreate the effect on new vehicles. Canadian Simon Deboer built this modern Jeep woody. (Courtesy Simon Deboer)

Index

Austin Bantam 4, 6, 38, 43
Austin Seven 38

Baker-Raulang 10, 18, 20
Blehl Body Co 4
Briggs 20
Budd Manufacturing Co 9
Buick 4, 5, 10, 19, 38, 48, 81-85

Cadillac 45, 48, 89
Cantrell 4, 10, 19, 48, 61, 72
Campbell 19
Chevrolet 4, 10-12, 14, 19, 35, 38-40, 42, 48, 67, 88, 72-75, 79
Chrysler 4, 7, 19, 32, 33, 35-37, 38, 51, 58, 60-65, 67, 69, 74, 87
Cotton 10
Crosley 86-88
Currier & Cameron Body Co 8

Daimler 8, 9,
DaimlerChrysler 88
DeSoto 4, 33, 66, 67
Dodge 4, 7, 9, 10, 19, 24, 28-32, 48, 59, 67, 68, 69, 72
Duesenberg 45
Durant 10, 18

Essex 10

Fisher Body 73, 79
Ford 4-6, 8, 10-28, 38, 48-59, 63, 75, 87

General Motors 19, 38, 63
GMC 72
Graham 38

Hercules 4, 10, 19, 42, 79
Hercules-Campbell 19
Hudson 44, 45
Hupp 38

International 4, 44, 45
Ionia Manufacturing Co 19
Ionia-Mitchell 4

Jeep 87, 89, 90
J H Mount 19
Jordon Motor Car Co. 19
Joseph Wildanger Company 19

Keller 87

LaSalle 49

www.velocebooks.com
Information on all books • New book news • Special offers • Gift vouchers

Index

Lincoln 5

Martin-Perry 10, 19
Maxwell 10
Marmon-Herrington 49
Mengel 20
Mercedes 8
Mercury 28, 51, 53-59, 87
Meteor 49, 59
Mid-State Body 19
Mifflinburg 10, 19, 42, 43
Murray Corporation 17, 20

Nash 86, 87

Oldsmobile 4, 8, 19, 48, 80, 81
Overland 10

Packard 38, 42, 43, 86, 87
Pierce-Arrow 9, 45
Playboy 87
Plymouth 4, 14, 24, 28, 31-34, 59, 67, 69-71

Pontiac 4, 19, 41, 42, 48, 76-79

Rambler 8
REO 10

Star 10
Seaman 10
Stanley 8
Stoughton Wagon Company 10
Studebaker 38, 87

Terraplane 46
Thomas 8

US Body & Forging 4, 28, 38, 48, 49

Waterloo Body Company 19
Willys 38, 44, 49

Ypsilanti Furniture Company 19
York 10

More *Those were the days ...* titles from Veloce Publishing –

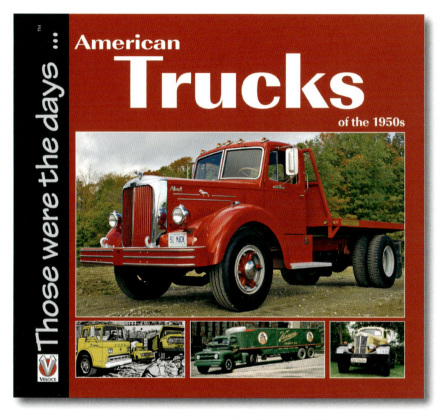

This highly visual study examines the important role of trucks and trucking in the 1950s, recounting the essential role it played in the industrial growth of the US and Canada. Features factory photos, advertisements, original truck brochures and restored examples, plus a comprehensive guide to all models produced.

$29.95/£14.99
ISBN: 978-1-84584-227-7

For more info on Veloce titles, visit our website at www.veloce.co.uk
email info@veloce.co.uk • tel: +44 (0)1305 260068 • prices subject to change • p+p extra

More *Those were the days ...* titles from Veloce Publishing –

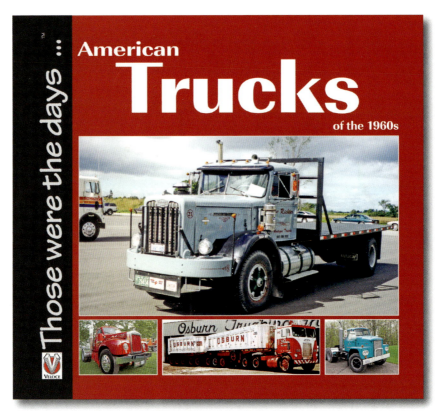

A highly visual study examines the important role of trucking in the growth of North America in the 1960s, when stiff competition led to failures and mergers. Features a comprehensive guide of all models produced.

$29.95/£14.99
ISBN: 978-1-84584-228-4

For more info on Veloce titles, visit our website at www.veloce.co.uk
email info@veloce.co.uk • tel: +44 (0)1305 260068 • prices subject to change • p+p extra

More *Those were the days ...* titles from Veloce Publishing –

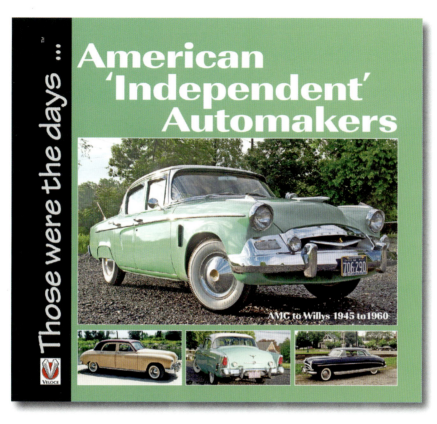

A highly visual look at the independent automakers who were the first to launch all-new models for a car-starved nation. Includes over 90 new, previously unpublished colour photos of restored examples relating the importance of these historic vehicles.

$29.95/£14.99
ISBN: 978-1-845842-39-0

For more info on Veloce titles, visit our website at www.veloce.co.uk
email info@veloce.co.uk • tel: +44 (0)1305 260068 • prices subject to change • p+p extra

More *Those were the days ...* titles from Veloce Publishing –

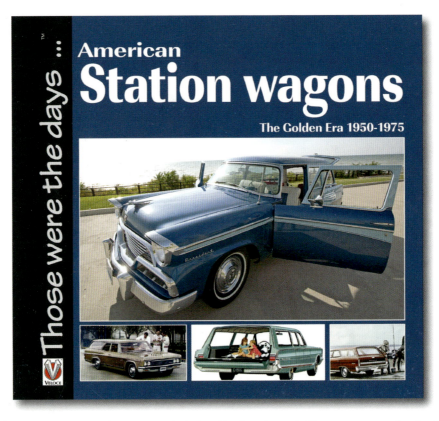

This book examines the important quarter century period when the American station wagon was a family standard and status symbol of a successful suburban lifestyle, recounting its essential role in North American society in the '50s, '60s and '70s.

$29.95/£14.99
ISBN: 978-1-845842-68-0

For more info on Veloce titles, visit our website at www.veloce.co.uk
email info@veloce.co.uk • tel: +44 (0)1305 260068 • prices subject to change • p+p extra